Jumpstarters for Geography

Short Daily Warm-ups for the Classroom

By
CINDY BARDEN

COPYRIGHT © 2007 Mark Twain Media, Inc.

ISBN 978-1-58037-401-9

Printing No. CD-404060

Mark Twain Media, Inc., Publishers
Distributed by Carson-Dellosa Publishing Company, Inc.

Table of Contents

** also includes Washington, D.C.

Introduction to the Teacher

Physical warm-ups help athletes prepare for more strenuous types of activity. Mental warm-ups help students prepare for the day's lesson while reviewing what they have previously learned.

The short warm-up activities presented in this book provide teachers and parents with activities to help students practice the skills they have already learned. Each page contains five warm-ups—one for each day of the school week. Used at the beginning of class, warm-ups help students focus on a geography-related topic. Activities are divided into four major regions with each region subdivided into smaller divisions as determined by the U.S. Census Bureau.

Geography is the study of the relationships between people, places, and environments and includes climate, weather, animals, plants, and features of land and sea. The warm-up activities include U.S. geography skills related to the states, their capitals and major cities, natural landforms and bodies of water, landmarks, parks, people of the regions, historical events, and other interesting features of the 50 U.S. states and Washington, D.C.

A set of maps included in the appendix can be copied for students' use with many activities. In addition to textbooks, students will find both printed and online reference sources, such as dictionaries, encyclopedias, atlases, and almanacs, to be useful reference tools.

Suggestions for use:

- Copy and cut apart one page each week. Give students one warm-up activity each day at the beginning of class.

- Give each student a copy of the entire page to complete day by day. Students can keep the completed pages in a three-ring binder or folder to use as a resource.

- Make transparencies of individual warm-ups and complete the activities as a group.

- Provide additional copies of warm-ups in your learning center for students to complete at random when they have a few extra minutes.

- Keep some warm-ups on hand to use as fill-ins when the class has a few extra minutes before lunch or dismissal.

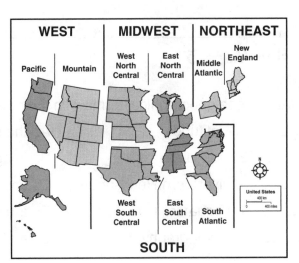

Geography Warm-ups: Using Maps

Name/Date _____

Using Maps 1

Compare a flat map of Earth to a globe. On your own paper, list three ways in which they are similar and three ways in which they are different.

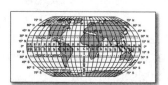

Name/Date _____

Using Maps 2

Answer the following questions on your own paper.

1. What is a compass rose?
2. What is a scale on a map?
3. The scale of maps are not always the same. Why not?
4. What is a map key?

Name/Date _____

Using Maps 3

Long ago, people drew maps in dirt to show the location of food, water, and other important places. Later, more permanent maps were painted on rocks, etched into clay tablets, or carved into wood. Today's maps are much more precise and varied and include interactive and three-dimensional maps. People driving from one state to another on vacation would find a road map useful so they don't get lost. On your own paper, list other examples of ways in which people use maps.

Name/Date _____

Using Maps 4

1. Use a dictionary to write a geographic definition for *continent*.

   _____

   _____

   _____

2. List the seven continents. _____

   _____

   _____

Name/Date _____

Using Maps 5

Match these geographical terms with their meanings.

_____ 1. latitude

_____ 2. longitude

_____ 3. Northern Hemisphere

_____ 4. equator

_____ 5. cartography

A. the study of and the construction of maps

B. imaginary lines circling Earth in an east/west direction

C. imaginary lines circling Earth in a north/south direction

D. the region of Earth north of the equator

E. an imaginary line around the middle of Earth

Geography Warm-ups: Using Maps (Appendix Map #1)

Name/Date _____

Using Maps 6

Use appendix map #1. Write an abbreviation for the correct direction to travel between the states listed. Use N; NE; E; SE; S; SW; W; or NW.

1. Wyoming to Montana _____   2. Idaho to California _____
3. Oklahoma to Tennessee _____   4. Utah to Arizona _____
5. Kansas to Iowa _____   6. Georgia to Mississippi _____
7. Alabama to Virginia _____   8. Texas to Oregon _____

Name/Date _____

Using Maps 7

Use appendix map #1. Lines of latitude run east and west; lines of longitude run north and south. Answer the following questions on your own paper.

1. What state would you be in if you were at 35° north latitude and 110° west longitude?
2. Is the location 30° north latitude and 120° west longitude on land or water?
3. How many states are completely north of 40° north latitude?

Name/Date _____

Using Maps 8

Select two pairs of capital cities and write them below. Use a ruler and the map scale to find the approximate distance between each pair of cities.

1. Between _____ and _____ = about _____ miles.
2. Between _____ and _____ = about _____ miles.

Name/Date _____

Using Maps 9

1. List three states that share a land or water border with Canada.

   _____

2. List three states that share a border with Mexico.

   _____

3. List three states that border on the Pacific Ocean.

   _____

Name/Date _____

Using Maps 10

Write N; NE; E; SE; S; SW; W; or NW for the correct direction to travel between the places listed.

1. Your home to the capital in your state _____
2. Your home to the Atlantic Ocean _____
3. Your home to the closest part of Canada _____
4. Your school to your home _____

3

Geography Warm-ups:
Using Maps (Appendix Map #1)

Name/Date _____

_____

Using Maps 11

Unscramble these words associated with maps.

1. lecsa

   _____

2. tedaluit

   _____

3. apcsoms

   _____

4. gdelen

   _____

5. olcitipla

   _____

6. sphliacy

   _____

7. niuedlgot

   _____

8. redsege

   _____

9. oesrdrb

   _____

10. nocase

   _____

Name/Date _____

Using Maps 12

1. List four states that border the Atlantic Ocean.

   _____   _____

   _____   _____

2. List four states that border the Gulf of Mexico.

   _____   _____

   _____   _____

Name/Date _____

Using Maps 13

1. Using an atlas or other source, list the five Great Lakes.

   _____   _____

   _____   _____

   _____

Name/Date _____

Using Maps 14

1. What direction would you travel to get from Florida to the state of Washington? _____

2. What direction would you travel to get from Minnesota to Louisiana? _____

Name/Date _____

Using Maps 15

1. List four states that border Missouri.

   _____   _____

   _____   _____

2. List four states that border West Virginia.

   _____   _____

   _____   _____

Geography Warm-ups: The Northeast New England States (Appendix Map #2)

Name/Date _____

New England 1

Write the names of the six New England states to match the numbers on appendix map #2.

1. _____   2. _____

3. _____   4. _____

5. _____   6. _____

Name/Date _____

New England 2

Write the names of the state capitals to match the numbers on appendix map #2.

1. _____   2. _____

3. _____   4. _____

5. _____   6. _____

Name/Date _____

New England 3

1. The windiest place in New England is Mount Washington, where winds have been clocked at over 200 mph. What state is home to Mount Washington? _____

2. Which New England state was the last of the 13 colonies to ratify the Constitution?

   _____

3. In which New England State did the Boston Tea Party take place? _____

4. Which New England state refused to join the United States after the Revolutionary War and declared itself an independent country with its own president, money, and postal service? _____

Name/Date _____

New England 4

Why do you think these states are referred to as New England states?

_____

_____

_____

_____

Name/Date _____

New England 5

Use appendix map #2 to answer the questions. Answer on your own paper.

1. What country is north of New England?
2. Which New England state is the farthest north?
3. Which body of water forms the eastern border of New England?
4. The smallest state in New England is also the smallest state in the U.S. What is it?

Geography Warm-ups: The Northeast New England States (Appendix Map #2)

Name/Date _____

_____

New England 6

Match the names of the states with their nicknames.

_____ 1. Connecticut

_____ 2. Massachusetts

_____ 3. Maine

_____ 4. New Hampshire

_____ 5. Rhode Island

_____ 6. Vermont

A. Bay State and Baked Bean State

B. Ocean State and Little Rhody

C. Green Mountain State

D. Nutmeg State and Constitution State

E. Granite State and White Mountain State

F. Pine Tree State

Name/Date _____

New England 7

Answer these questions on your own paper.
1. Use a dictionary or other source to define a **cape** as a geographical feature.
2. Which of the New England states has the longest cape extending into the Atlantic Ocean? What is its name?
3. Use any source to find this answer: How did Cape Cod get its name?

Name/Date _____

New England 8

1. What mountain range runs through much of New England? _____

2. Which Canadian province forms part of the eastern border of Maine? _____
3. For what type of soup is New England famous? _____

Name/Date _____

New England 9

Cross out the types of plants that would not grow naturally outdoors in New England.

| Maple | Pine | Palm | Grapefruit |
| Oak | Bamboo | Orchids | Roses |

Name/Date _____

New England 10

Many Native American tribes lived in New England before settlers arrived from Europe. Select any group from that area and write a short report about them on another sheet of paper.

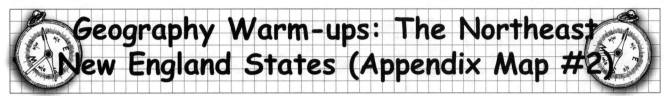

Geography Warm-ups: The Northeast New England States (Appendix Map #2)

Name/Date _____

New England 11

Circle "T" for true or "F" for false.

1. T   F   Maine was one of the original 13 colonies.
2. T   F   Maine is well-known for its long stretches of smooth sandy beaches along the Atlantic Ocean.
3. T   F   West Quoddy Head in Maine is the easternmost point of land on the U.S. mainland.
4. T   F   The Cadillac Mountains are in Acadia National Park.
5. T   F   Sea mammals like seals, porpoises, and whales live along Maine's coast.

Name/Date _____

New England 12

1. Which Canadian province forms part of the border of New Hampshire?

    _____

2. What was the name of the famous rock formation in the White Mountains of New Hampshire that looked like an old man's head? _____

3. What happened to it in 2003? _____
    _____

Name/Date _____

New England 13

1. The French explorer Samuel de Champlain named the area *vert mont*. What does that mean in English? _____

    _____

2. Ethan Allen and his Green Mountain Boys were soldiers in which war?

    _____

3. What river forms the eastern boundary of Vermont? _____

Name/Date _____

New England 14

Answer these questions on your own paper.
1. The Puritans established the Connecticut Colony as a theocracy. What is a theocracy?
2. Which city first flourished as a whaling port and is now home to the P. T. Barnum Museum?
3. Founded in Bradford, Connecticut, in 1701, Yale University moved to which city four years later?

Name/Date _____

New England 15

Use reference sources. Write five interesting facts about Rhode Island on another sheet of paper. Share what you learned with the class.

The quahog is the state shell of Rhode Island.

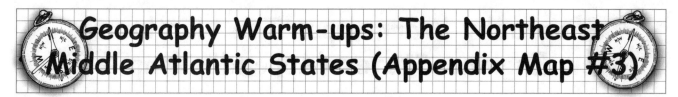

Geography Warm-ups: The Northeast Middle Atlantic States (Appendix Map #3)

Name/Date _____

Middle Atlantic States 1

Write the names of the three Middle Atlantic States and their capitals to match the numbers on appendix map #3.

	States	**Capitals**
1.	_____	_____
2.	_____	_____
3.	_____	_____

Name/Date _____

Middle Atlantic States 2

Use appendix map #3 or another reference source to answer these questions. Write the answers on your own paper.

1. Which Middle Atlantic state is farthest north?
2. Which states share the southern border of Pennsylvania?
3. Which two Great Lakes border the Middle Atlantic states?

Name/Date _____

Middle Atlantic States 3

1. Use a dictionary or other source to define *climate*. _____
_____

2. Based on climate, circle the animals likely to be found in the Middle Atlantic states.

    deer   parrots   alligators

    raccoons   eagles   turkeys

    lizards   polar bears   frogs

Name/Date _____

Middle Atlantic States 4

Use appendix map #3 or other sources to answer the questions.

1. Which of the Middle Atlantic States is the largest in area? _____

2. Based on location, is the climate of the Middle Atlantic states generally warmer or colder than Florida? _____

3. Which river forms the boundary between New Jersey and Pennsylvania? _____

Name/Date _____

Middle Atlantic States 5

1. The name of which Pennsylvania city comes from a Greek term meaning "city of brotherly love"? _____

2. Pittsburgh was originally the site of which British fort? _____

3. What is the official name of the state of Pennsylvania? _____

4. For whom was the state named? _____

5. What does Pennsylvania mean? _____

Geography Warm-ups: The Northeast Middle Atlantic States (Appendix Map #3)

Name/Date _____

Middle Atlantic States 6

Answer the following questions on your own paper.
1. What was the Dutch name for New York City?
2. What city in New York was the capital of the United States from 1785 to 1790?
3. What is the name of the large island that is part of New York?
4. What is the name of the park that covers about 840 acres in the center of Manhattan?

Name/Date _____

Middle Atlantic States 7

Match these places with their nicknames.

_____ 1. New York City, NY   A. Empire State
_____ 2. Pittsburgh, PA   B. Garden State
_____ 3. New Jersey   C. Keystone State
_____ 4. Pennsylvania   D. Big Apple
_____ 5. New York   E. Steel City

Name/Date _____

Middle Atlantic States 8

The official state song of New York is "I Love New York." Neither New Jersey nor Pennsylvania has an official state song. Work with a partner to make up a short song, chant, or rap for Pennsylvania or New Jersey. Write it on another sheet of paper.

Name/Date _____

Middle Atlantic States 9

On another sheet of paper, make a chart showing the official state motto, flower, tree, animal, bird, and insect for Pennsylvania, New Jersey, and New York.

Name/Date _____

Middle Atlantic States 10

1. The first known inhabitants of New Jersey were part of the Delaware tribe who called themselves the

_____,

which means "original people."

2. Which country was the first to claim ownership of the area around New Jersey, based on the explorations of Henry Hudson?

_____

3. Born in Newark, New Jersey, he became vice president under Thomas Jefferson, but is better known for his duel with Alexander Hamilton in 1804. Who was he?

_____

4. After General Washington crossed the ice-filled Delaware River with his troops on December 25, 1776, an important Revolutionary War battle took place. Name the New Jersey site of this battle.

_____

Geography Warm-ups: The Midwest, East North Central States (Appendix Map #4)

Name/Date _____

East North Central States 1

Write the names of the five Midwestern states to match the numbers on appendix map #4.

1. _____
2. _____
3. _____
4. _____
5. _____

Name/Date _____

East North Central States 2

Write the names of the state capitals to match the numbers on appendix map #4.

1. _____
2. _____
3. _____
4. _____
5. _____

Name/Date _____

East North Central States 3

Why do you think these states are referred to as Midwestern states?

_____

_____

_____

_____

_____

Name/Date _____

East North Central States 4

Use appendix map #4 and other sources to answer these questions.

1. Which of the Midwestern states in this region extends the farthest north? _____
2. Which of these states is the farthest east? _____
3. Which of these states extends the farthest south? _____
4. Which of these states border the Mississippi River? _____

Name/Date _____

East North Central States 5

Use a dictionary or other source.

1. What is a peninsula? _____

   _____

2. Which of the Midwestern states has a large peninsula extending into two of the Great Lakes?

   _____

3. Although it is part of one state, this peninsula, known as the Upper Peninsula (UP), is actually attached to another state. To which state is the UP attached? _____

Geography Warm-ups: The Midwest East North Central States (Appendix Map #4)

Name/Date _____

East North Central States 6

1. Write the names of the four Great Lakes that touch states in the East North Central area of the Midwest. _____

2. What is the name of the fifth Great Lake that does not border this area? _____

3. Which of the Great Lakes is farthest north? _____

4. Which of the Great Lakes is farthest east? _____

5. Which of the Great Lakes is totally within the United States? _____

6. The United States and which country share a border with four of the Great Lakes? _____

Name/Date _____

East North Central States 7

Answer these questions on your own paper.

1. What caused the formation of the Great Lakes?

2. What does the word *lake* mean?

3. Why are these five lakes called "great" lakes?

Name/Date _____

East North Central States 8

Answer these questions on your own paper.

1. Use the map scale on a larger map, a ruler, and a piece of string to find the approximate distance by water from Chicago, Illinois, to Montreal, Canada.

2. Along the route, it was sometimes necessary to portage canoes and goods for a time. What does *portage* mean?

3. What product did French explorers send back to Europe from this area in the mid-1500s to 1700s?

Name/Date _____

East North Central States 9

1. Which Midwestern city is nicknamed the "Windy City"? _____

2. Which Midwestern city is nicknamed the "Motor City"? _____

3. Which Midwestern city houses the Pro Football Hall of Fame? _____

4. True or False? All of the area in this part of the Midwest was part of the Louisiana Purchase in 1803. _____

Name/Date _____

East North Central States 10

Select the nickname for one of these Midwestern states and explain how that state got its nickname. Write your answer on another sheet of paper.

Geography Warm-ups: The Midwest, East North Central States (Appendix Map #4)

Name/Date _____

_____

East North Central States 11

Write the name of the word associated with Ohio that matches each definition below.

Akron	**Cincinnati**
Dayton	**Ohio**
Toledo	

1. From an Iroquois word meaning "something great" or "beautiful"

   _____

2. Home of the Red Stockings, baseball's oldest professional team

   _____

3. Means "high point" in Greek

   _____

4. Named for a city in Spain

   _____

5. Home of Wilbur and Orville Wright

   _____

Name/Date _____

East North Central States 12

Answer these questions on your own paper.
1. What does the word *Indiana* mean?
2. In the early 1900s, what industry in Indiana produced Duesenbergs, Auburns, Stutzes, and Maxwells?
3. In which Indiana city can visitors view a reproduction of the *Santa Maria*?
4. Which river is the longest in the state of Indiana and forms part of the western border between Indiana and Illinois?

Name/Date _____

East North Central States 13

1. The first modern skyscraper was built in Chicago in 1885. How tall was it? _____
2. People of the Hopewell Culture were mound builders who lived in the area between 300 B.C. and A.D. 500. Who were the other group of mound builders who lived there between A.D. 800 and 1500? _____

Name/Date _____

East North Central States 14

Answer these questions on your own paper.
1. Chief Pontiac's efforts to drive the Europeans from the region ended in defeat. What was the name of his tribe?
2. True or False? The word *Michigan* came from a Chippewa word meaning "sunny hills."
3. The Straits of Mackinac connect Lake Michigan and Lake Huron. What is a strait?

Name/Date _____

East North Central States 15

1. What are two nicknames for Wisconsin? _____

   _____

2. What is the largest lake totally inside the boundaries of Wisconsin? _____
3. Which group of Native Americans called themselves the *mesquaki*, meaning "the red earth people," and lived on the shore at Lake Butte des Mortes? _____

Geography Warm-ups: The Midwest, West North Central States (Appendix Map #5)

Name/Date _____

West North Central States 1

Write the names of the seven West North Central Midwestern states to match the numbers on appendix map #5.

1. _____   2. _____
3. _____   4. _____
5. _____   6. _____
7. _____

Name/Date _____

West North Central States 2

Write the names of the state capitals to match the numbers on appendix map #5.

1. _____   2. _____
3. _____   4. _____
5. _____   6. _____
7. _____

Name/Date _____

West North Central States 3

Use appendix map #5. Circle "T" for true or "F" for false.

1. T   F   North Dakota and South Dakota share their borders with Canada.
2. T   F   Missouri is the state that extends the farthest south and east in this region.
3. T   F   The Mississippi River forms part of the boundary between Iowa and Missouri.
4. T   F   South Dakota is west of Iowa.
5. T   F   Kansas is southwest of Minnesota.

Name/Date _____

West North Central States 4

The states in this part of the Midwest (except Missouri) are often called the Great Plains States. Answer these questions on your own paper.

1. What is the geographical meaning of *plain*?
2. Early American settlers in the Great Plains area often built sod houses. Why?
3. Describe a sod house and how it was built.

Name/Date _____

West North Central States 5

Answer these questions on your own paper.

1. Which states in this region border Lake Superior?
2. What major river flows through the region and joins the Mississippi River?
3. What is the name of the body of water where the Mississippi River ends?
4. Which state is sometimes called the Land of 10,000 Lakes?

13

Geography Warm-ups: The Midwest, West North Central States (Appendix Map #5)

Name/Date _____

West North Central States 6

Consider the climate of the Midwest. Circle the types of crops that would probably grow well there:

wheat	coconuts	pineapples
apples	soybeans	bananas
corn	potatoes	cabbage
rice	hay	sugar cane

Name/Date _____

West North Central States 7

Number the seven states in this area by size from largest to smallest, with 1 being the largest.

____ South Dakota   ____ North Dakota

____ Nebraska   ____ Missouri

____ Minnesota   ____ Kansas

____ Iowa

Name/Date _____

West North Central States 8

Match the states with their nicknames.

____ 1. South Dakota A. Cornhusker State

____ 2. North Dakota B. Sunflower State

____ 3. Nebraska   C. Show-Me State

____ 4. Missouri   D. Hawkeye State

____ 5. Minnesota   E. Gopher State

____ 6. Kansas   F. Peace Garden State

____ 7. Iowa   G. Coyote State

Name/Date _____

West North Central States 9

Answer these questions on your own paper.
1. From fossil evidence, scientists know that Nebraska once had a tropical climate. Briefly describe the present climate in Nebraska.
2. In 1819, the first military fort west of the Mississippi River was built. Name it.
3. Near what city and in what year did Father Flanagan found Boys Town?
4. The word Nebraska comes from an Oto word, *nebrathka*. What does it mean?

Name/Date _____

West North Central States 10

Answer these questions on your own paper.
1. When did Iowa become a state?
2. The two main agricultural products in Iowa are corn and soybeans. From corn we get corn syrup, corn meal, and many other products. List at least five other products made from corn.
3. From soybeans we get both edible products and industrial products, including oil used in margarine and mayonnaise, as well as paint, varnish, and linoleum. List at least five other products made from soybeans.
4. True or False? Iowa means "the beautiful land" in the Ioway language.
5. True or False? Chief Black Hawk was a famous Sauk leader who led an unsuccessful rebellion against settlers in 1832.

Geography Warm-ups: The Midwest West North Central States (Appendix Map #5)

Name/Date _____

West North Central States 11

Match the term with the correct definition.

____ 1. Lake Itasca

____ 2. International Falls

____ 3. Eagle Mountain

____ 4. Minnesota

A. A Dakota word meaning "sky-tinted"

B. Source of the Mississippi River

C. Nicknamed "The Nation's Icebox"

D. Highest point in Minnesota

Name/Date _____

West North Central States 12

Answer these questions on your own paper.

1. The author of *The Adventures of Tom Sawyer* was from Hannibal, MO. What was his name?

2. Earthquakes near _____, MO, in 1811 and 1812 caused the Mississippi River to temporarily flow backwards.

3. Pony Express service operated between Sacramento, CA, and _____.

4. The Ozark Plateau region is also called the Ozark Mountains. What is a *plateau*?

Name/Date _____

West North Central States 13

Write "SD" and/or "ND" to indicate South Dakota or North Dakota.

1. State bird is the western meadowlark. _____

2. State fish is the walleye. _____

3. Site of the Black Hills _____

4. Mount Rushmore state _____

5. State flower is the wild prairie rose. _____

6. Home of the Badlands _____

7. Home of the International Peace Garden _____

8. State drink is milk. _____

9. Coyote is the state animal. _____

10. Home of the Corn Palace _____

Name/Date _____

West North Central States 14

Thousands of limestone caves are located in Missouri. Write your answers on another sheet of paper.

1. What is a cave?

2. How large are caves?

3. What is limestone?

4. How are limestone caves formed?

5. What is a stalactite?

6. What is a stalagmite?

Name/Date _____

West North Central States 15

Kansas was home to many U.S. forts including Forts Hays, Larned, Dodge, Harker, Zarah, Wallace, Leavenworth, Scott, and Riley. On another sheet of paper, describe one Kansas fort; where, when, and why it was built; and what it is like today.

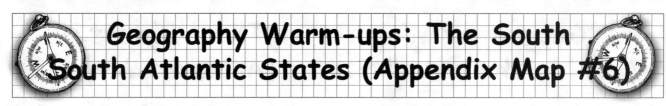

Geography Warm-ups: The South
South Atlantic States (Appendix Map #6)

Name/Date _____

South Atlantic States 1

Write the names of the eight South Atlantic states to match the numbers on appendix map #6.

1. _____   2. _____
3. _____   4. _____
5. _____   6. _____
7. _____   8. _____

9. Put an * by the names of the states listed above that were not part of the original 13 states.

Name/Date _____

South Atlantic States 2

Write the names of the state capitals to match the numbers on appendix map #6.

1. _____   2. _____
3. _____   4. _____
5. _____   6. _____
7. _____   8. _____

Name/Date _____

South Atlantic States 3

Use appendix map #6. Circle "T" for true or "F" for false.

1. T F The Atlantic Ocean borders the South Atlantic states on the east.

2. T F Florida is the southernmost state in this area and in the entire U.S.

3. T F North Carolina is located between Georgia and South Carolina.

Name/Date _____

South Atlantic States 4

Answer the questions on your own paper.
1. Which two states border Chesapeake Bay?
2. What is a bay?
3. Which state in this region borders the Gulf of Mexico?
4. What is a gulf?
5. What are the Florida Keys?

Name/Date _____

South Atlantic States 5

Answer the questions on your own paper.

1. What area in this region is not part of any state?

2. Washington, D.C., was chosen as the capital of the United States in 1790 because of its central location. If you were to choose a centrally located place for the country's capital today, where would it be?

3. True or False? The D.C. in Washington, D.C., stands for District of Columbus.

4. You can't go shopping at the Mall in Washington, D.C. Why not?

5. Which river runs through Washington, D.C.?

6. True or False? By 1800, Washington, D.C., was a large, prosperous city with paved roads, many large beautiful homes, and an efficient sanitation system.

16

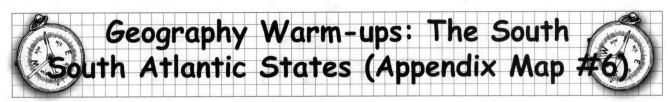

Geography Warm-ups: The South
South Atlantic States (Appendix Map #6)

Name/Date _____

South Atlantic States 6

For each pair of states listed, circle the one that is larger.

1. Delaware or Maryland
2. Virginia or West Virginia
3. North Carolina or South Carolina
4. Georgia or Florida
5. West Virginia or South Carolina
6. North Carolina or Virginia

Name/Date _____

South Atlantic States 7

Answer these on your own paper.

1. Which of the South Atlantic States do not border the Atlantic Ocean?
2. Which mountain range extends over most of the South Atlantic States?
3. What other mountain range, considered part of this range, is primarily in West Virginia?
4. West Virginia has vast deposits of coal. How is coal formed?

Name/Date _____

South Atlantic States 8

1. Dover is the capital, but the largest city in Delaware is _____.
2. Why is Delaware called "The First State"?
   _____
   _____
3. Led by Peter Minuit, colonists from The Netherlands and _____ formed the first permanent European settlement in Delaware at Fort Christina.

Name/Date _____

South Atlantic States 9

Answer these on your own paper.

1. For whom was Maryland named?

2. What is the Mason-Dixon Line?

3. The *skipjack* is Maryland's official state boat. On another sheet of paper, draw or describe a skipjack.

Name/Date _____

South Atlantic States 10

1. Cape Hatteras is located off the coast of _____.
2. In 1587, more than 100 settlers disappeared from this island. _____
3. The islands of Hilton Head, Sullivans, Parris, St. Helena, and Daufuskie are part of the state of

   _____.

4. _____ was claimed by Juan Ponce de León for Spain in 1513.
5. Ossabaw Sound, St. Catherines Sound, and Sapelo Sound are three sounds off the coast of Georgia. What is the geographical meaning of *sound*? _____

   _____

Geography Warm-ups: The South
South Atlantic States (Appendix Map #6)

Name/Date _____

South Atlantic States 11

Match the place below with the correct definition.

_____	1.	Ocracoke Island	A. Site of the Wright brothers' first airplane flight
_____	2.	Bath	B. Named for the wife of King George III
_____	3.	New Bern	C. Named for a city in England
_____	4.	Charlotte	D. Named for a city in Switzerland
_____	5.	Tuscaroras	E. A group of Native Americans
_____	6.	Kitty Hawk	F. Hideout of Edward Teach (Blackbeard)

Name/Date _____

South Atlantic States 12
Answer these questions on your own paper.
1. West Virginia was once part of what other state?
2. In 1861, West Virginia voted against secession from the Union. It became a separate state in what year?
3. West Virginia has a rather odd shape. Why do you think the two parts in the north that stick out are called panhandles?
4. Why did King George III ban further settlements west of the Alleghenies in 1763?

Name/Date _____

South Atlantic States 13

List the state symbols for South Carolina on another sheet of paper.

1.	State motto	2.	State flower
3.	State bird	4.	State fruit
5.	State beverage	6.	State dance
7.	State dog	8.	State insect
9.	State reptile	10.	State fish
11.	State stone	12.	State wild game bird

Name/Date _____

South Atlantic States 14

Circle "T" for true or "F" for false.
1. T F One nickname for Georgia is "The Goober State." Goobers are peanuts.
2. T F James Oglethorpe formed a plan to resettle debtors in America.
3. T F Georgia is 600 miles long (north to south) and 500 miles wide (east to west).
4. T F Cotton, peaches, and peanuts are major crops in Georgia.

Name/Date _____

South Atlantic States 15
1. Most of southern Florida (2,746 square miles) is covered by two huge marshy areas called the _____ and the _____.
2. On another sheet of paper, list at least 25 plants and animals commonly found in Florida's swamps.
3. A series of wars was fought in the mid-1800s by the United States against which Native American group who lived mainly in the swamps of Florida?
   _____

Geography Warm-ups: The South East South Central States (Appendix Map #7)

Name/Date _____

East South Central States 1

Write the names of the four East South Central States and their capitals to match the numbers on appendix map #7.

	State	Capital
1.	_____	_____
2.	_____	_____
3.	_____	_____
4.	_____	_____

Name/Date _____

East South Central States 2

Answer these questions on your own paper.

1. Which states in this region border on the Gulf of Mexico?
2. Which states in this region border on the Mississippi River?
3. Which seven states share a border with Kentucky?
4. Which state in this region is the farthest north?
5. Which river forms most of the northern border of Kentucky?

Name/Date _____

East South Central States 3

Unscramble the letters to find the names of two major cities for each state. Write the answers on your own paper.

1. Kentucky: A. tongelinx   B. vileussoill
2. Tennessee: A. agonotcatha   B. hispmme
3. Alabama: A. hiveuntsll   B. hambingirm
4. Mississippi: A. theznca   B. ibxloi

Name/Date _____

East South Central States 4

Match the year in which each of these states entered the Union.

1792   1796   1817   1819

1. _____ Alabama   2. _____ Kentucky
3. _____ Mississippi   4. _____ Tennessee
5. For many years, when _____ was "king," people in Alabama and Mississippi raised only this one major cash crop.

Name/Date _____

_____

East South Central States 5

Write "AL" for Alabama, "KY" for Kentucky, "MS" for Mississippi, or "TN" for Tennessee to match the states with the facts.

_____ 1. State bird is the mockingbird.
_____ 2. State animal is the raccoon.
_____ 3. State fruit is the blackberry.
_____ 4. State flower is the magnolia.
_____ 5. State bird is the cardinal.
_____ 6. State bird is the yellowhammer.
_____ 7. State flower is the iris.
_____ 8. State game bird is the wild turkey.
_____ 9. State insect is the firefly.
_____ 10. State marine mammal is the bottlenose dolphin.

19

Geography Warm-ups: The South East South Central States (Appendix Map #7)

Name/Date _____

East South Central States 6

Circle "T" for true or "F" for false.
1. T F The Kentucky Derby is actually held in Tennessee.
2. T F The largest natural lake in Tennessee, Reelfoot Lake, formed after earthquakes in 1811 and 1812.
3. T F People in Enterprise, Alabama, built the Boll Weevil Monument in 1910 after that insect destroyed most of the state's cotton crop.

Name/Date _____

East South Central States 7

Answer these questions on your own paper.
1. The south central part of Kentucky is called the Pennyroyal region. What is a pennyroyal?
2. The north central part of Kentucky is known as the Bluegrass region. What color is Kentucky bluegrass?
3. Cumberland Falls is famous for its moonbows. What is a moonbow?
4. Mammoth Cave is part of the longest cave system on Earth. How long is it?

Name/Date _____

East South Central States 8

Answer these questions on your own paper.
1. The Trail of Tears went from northern Georgia through Tennessee, western Kentucky, southern Illinois, then across Missouri to Oklahoma. What was the Trail of Tears?
2. The earliest people known to settle in Tennessee arrived about 15,000 years ago. Why have they been named the Mound Builders?
3. What was the name of the Cherokee chief who developed a written alphabet for his people?

Name/Date _____

East South Central States 9

Answer these questions on your own paper.
1. Huge petrified trees have been found in Mississippi. How does wood become petrified?
2. One nickname for Mississippi is "The Mud-Cat State." What is a mud cat?
3. Jackson was built on the bluffs of the Pearl River. What are bluffs?
4. Why was the lighthouse at Biloxi painted black after the Civil War?

Name/Date _____

East South Central States 10

1. The first European explorers in Alabama came from _____ in the early 1500s.
2. Which Alabama tribe of Native Americans was defeated by General Andrew Jackson in 1814? _____
3. The city of Tuscaloosa was named for a Native American chief of the _____ tribe.
4. _____ became the birthplace of the Civil Rights Movement in 1955.
5. _____ was sworn in as President of the Confederate States of America in Montgomery on February 18, 1861.

Geography Warm-ups: The South
West South Central States (Appendix Map #8)

Name/Date _____

West South Central States 1

Write the names of the four West South Central States and their capitals to match the numbers on appendix map #8.

	State	Capital
1.	_____	_____
2.	_____	_____
3.	_____	_____
4.	_____	_____

Name/Date _____

West South Central States 2

Answer these questions on your own paper.
1. Tornadoes and hurricanes are weather systems that frequently affect this region of the United States. Which major hurricane hit in 2005, devastating many major cities, including New Orleans?
2. Texas and Oklahoma are part of the area known as "Tornado Alley." Briefly explain the difference between a hurricane and a tornado.

Name/Date _____

West South Central States 3

1. Which state's name came from two Choctaw words meaning "red men"?

   _____

2. What does Rio Grande mean in English? _____

3. Which state's name came from a Caddo Indian word meaning "friends"? _____

4. Louisiana was named for King Louis XIV. What country did he rule? _____

5. Baton Rouge means "red stick" in English. How did it get its name? _____

   _____

Name/Date _____

West South Central States 4

1. Which large body of water borders this region on the southeast? _____
2. Which of these four states is the largest?

   _____
3. What country borders Texas on the southwest?

   _____
4. Most states are subdivided into smaller units called counties. What are the smaller units called in Louisiana? _____

Name/Date _____

West South Central States 5

Answer these questions on your own paper.
1. The highest point in Oklahoma is Black Mesa at 4,973 feet above sea level. What is a mesa?
2. Although much of Oklahoma is plains, there are mountains in the state. Name three mountain ranges in Oklahoma.
3. Which river forms the southern border between Oklahoma and Texas?
4. List the Oklahoma state animal, amphibian, fish, bird, and tree.

Geography Warm-ups: The South
West South Central States (Appendix Map #8)

Name/Date _____

West South Central States 6

Match the correct definition to each term.

_____ 1. Levee   A. Above-ground cemeteries

_____ 2. Nutria   B. Descendents of people from Spain or France and African slaves

_____ 3. Creoles   C. A high bank or dike to protect land from flooding

_____ 4. Cajuns   D. Another name for a coypu (a large rodent)

_____ 5. Cities of the Dead   E. Descendents of people originally from the French Acadia colony in Canada

---

Name/Date _____

West South Central States 7

Answer these questions on your own paper.

1. One unofficial nickname for Arkansas is "The Razorback State." What is a razorback?
2. Near what city in Arkansas is the only active diamond mine in North America?
3. Hot Springs National Park includes 47 hot mineral springs. What is a hot spring?

Name/Date _____

West South Central States 8

Circle "T" for true or "F" for false.

1. T F Padre Island National Seashore is an area of beaches and sand dunes in southeastern Texas.
2. T F Texas was once an independent country.
3. T F Texas is the largest of the 50 states.
4. T F Corpus Christi, Galveston, Dallas, and Austin are major port cities in Texas.
5. T F Millions of bats live in Bracken Cave near San Antonio.

Name/Date _____

West South Central States 9

1. The Texas Rangers were first organized by _____ in 1823 to protect Americans from attacks by the Comanche and Apache.
2. When was the Republic of Texas formed? _____ Who was its first president? _____ How long was it an independent country? _____

Name/Date _____

West South Central States 10

Answer these questions on your own paper.

1. The Mississippi River delta and wetlands area are part of Southern Louisiana. What is a delta?
2. What are wetlands?
3. Louisiana is called "The Bayou State." What is a bayou?
4. The lowest point in the state is eight feet below sea level. What is sea level?

Geography Warm-ups: The West Mountain States (Appendix Map #9)

Name/Date _____

Mountain States 1

Write the names of the eight Mountain states to match the numbers on appendix map #9.

1. _____   2. _____
3. _____   4. _____
5. _____   6. _____
7. _____   8. _____

Name/Date _____

Mountain States 2

Write the names of the state capitals to match the numbers on appendix map #9.

1. _____   2. _____
3. _____   4. _____
5. _____   6. _____
7. _____   8. _____

Name/Date _____

Mountain States 3

Write the name of the state to match its nickname.

1. Treasure State: _____   7. Silver State: _____
2. Grand Canyon State: _____   8. Centennial State: _____
3. Beehive State: _____
4. Land of Enchantment: _____
5. Gem State: _____
6. Equality State: _____

Name/Date _____

Mountain States 4

1. Which Mountain states share a border with Mexico? _____
2. In which state is the Grand Canyon? _____
3. In which state is the Great Salt Lake located? _____
4. Which Mountain states share a border with Canada? _____
5. Where is Yellowstone National Park located? _____

Name/Date _____

Mountain States 5

Answer these questions on your own paper.

1. Hells Canyon in Idaho and Oregon is the deepest canyon in North America. What is a canyon?
2. Why are the borders of some states straight lines and some very crooked lines?
3. Which major mountain range runs from north to south through the Mountain states?
4. Which Mountain states are not in the Mountain time zone?

23

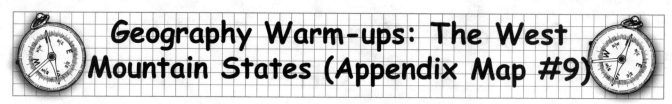

Geography Warm-ups: The West Mountain States (Appendix Map #9)

Name/Date _____

Mountain States 6

1. I am at a place called "Four Corners." Where am I? _____

2. I am watching a geyser called "Old Faithful." Where am I? _____

3. I am exploring Cliff Palace, where the Anasazi once lived. Where am I? _____

4. I am standing near a natural rock formation that was the first national monument established by the U.S. in 1906. Where am I? _____

Name/Date _____

Mountain States 7

Write the two-letter abbreviations for the states to match the state birds.

1. ___ lark bunting

2. ___ and ___ mountain bluebird

3. ___ cactus wren

4. ___ roadrunner

5. ___ California gull

6. ___ and ___ western meadowlark

Name/Date _____

Mountain States 8

1. Idaho became a state in what year: 1795, 1890, or 1915? _____

2. Two-thirds of the world's supply of which crop grows in Idaho: tomatoes, potatoes, peaches, or apples? _____

3. Idaho is first in the nation in the production of gold, silver, or diamonds? _____

4. What is the state fruit of Idaho: huckleberry, cherry, or apple? _____

Name/Date _____

Mountain States 9

Circle "T" for true or "F" for false.

1. T F   Montana means "mountain" in Spanish.

2. T F   There are about three times more cattle than people in Montana.

3. T F   Montana has the lowest population density of any state.

4. T F   The chinooks are cold winds that blow across Montana in the summer.

5. T F   The northern border of Montana is over 1,000 miles long.

Name/Date _____

Mountain States 10

On another sheet of paper, define the underlined words in this paragraph.

Yellowstone National Park became the first national park in 1872. Much of Yellowstone sits inside an ancient volcanic caldera (the exploded crater of a volcano). This area is known for spectacular snowcapped mountains, huge lakes, geysers, waterfalls, hot springs, deep canyons, abundant wildlife, and fossil forests. It contains more than 10,000 thermal sites such as geysers, hot springs, mud pots, and fumaroles.

24

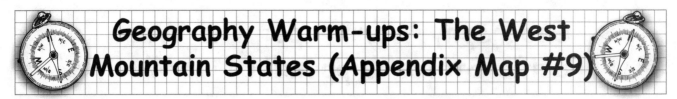

Geography Warm-ups: The West Mountain States (Appendix Map #9)

Name/Date _____

Mountain States 11

Answer these questions on your own paper.
1. Which religious group founded Salt Lake City in 1847?
2. Great Salt Lake is seven times saltier than the ocean. Why is it salty?
3. What caused the formation of so many beautiful spires and pinnacles in Bryce Canyon National Park?
4. How were the arches and bridges of Arches National Park in eastern Utah formed?

Name/Date _____

Mountain States 12

1. T   F   More than 1,000 peaks in Colorado are more than two miles high.
2. T   F   The first gold strike in Colorado occurred in 1838, 10 years before the famous gold rush in California.
3. T   F   Sand dunes in the Great Sand Dunes National Monument cover about 40 square miles and can reach 700 feet in height.

Name/Date _____

Mountain States 13

Answer these questions on your own paper.
1. Phoenix is the capital of Arizona. In mythology, what is a phoenix?
2. Why do you think someone would name a city after a phoenix?
3. The Hopi lived in pueblos. What are pueblos, and why are they appropriate to a desert climate?

Name/Date _____

Mountain States 14

Describe these New Mexico-related words on another sheet of paper.

1. adobe
2. kiva
3. petroglyph
4. Carlsbad Caverns
5. javelina
6. piñon tree
7. butte
8. saguaro

Name/Date _____

_____

Mountain States 15

1. What is unusual about Lake Mead?

_____

_____

_____

_____

2. Lake Tahoe is the second largest and second deepest alpine lake in North America. In what mountain range is Lake Tahoe?

_____

3. Write a brief report about one of these beautiful natural features of Nevada on another sheet of paper.

• Pyramid Lake
• Great Basin National Park
• Lehman Caves
• Humboldt National Forest
• the Valley of Fire
• Cathedral Gorge
• Lunar Crater
• Paradise Valley
• Berlin-Ichthyosaur State Park

Geography Warm-ups: The West Pacific States (Appendix Map #10)

Name/Date _____

Pacific States 1

Write the names of the five Pacific states and their capitals to match the numbers on appendix map #10.

	State	**Capital**
1.	_____	_____
2.	_____	_____
3.	_____	_____
4.	_____	_____
5.	_____	_____

Name/Date _____

Pacific States 2

1. Which two states are not part of the continental United States?

   _____

2. Which of the Pacific states is the farthest north? _____

3. Which direction would you go to get from California to Mexico? _____

4. Which direction would you travel to get from Hawaii to Alaska? _____

Name/Date _____

Pacific States 3

1. Which river forms much of the border between Washington and Oregon? _____

2. Which two states had major gold rushes?

   _____

3. Which Pacific states share a border with Canada? _____

   _____

4. Which Pacific state shares a border with Mexico? _____

Name/Date _____

Pacific States 4

Write the two-letter abbreviation of the Pacific state(s) where you would be likely to see the following.

_____ 1. a kookaburra in a tree

_____ 2. a moose and a grizzly bear at a creek

_____ 3. a pineapple plantation

_____ 4. salmon swimming upstream

_____ 5. a glacier

_____ 6. forest of sequoia trees

Name/Date _____

Pacific States 5

Write the two-letter abbreviation of the state to match the location of each body of water.

_____ 1. Bering Sea

_____ 3. Kauai Channel

_____ 5. Norton Sound

_____ 7. Monterey Bay

_____ 9. Strait of Juan de Fuca

_____ 11. Keehi Lagoon

_____ 2. Willapa Bay

_____ 4. Kamishak Bay

_____ 6. Coos Bay

_____ 8. Puget Sound

_____ 10. Crater Lake

_____ 12. Gray's Harbor

Geography Warm-ups: The West Pacific States (Appendix Map #10)

Name/Date _____

Pacific States 6

Circle "T" for true or "F" for false.

1. T F Juneau, Alaska, is the northernmost city in the U.S.
2. T F There are only 12 letters in the Hawaiian alphabet.
3. T F After gold was discovered in California, the population rapidly increased from about 26,000 to 100,000.
4. T F Mount Shasta is a volcano in Washington.
5. T F The Oregon Donation Land Law of 1850 granted 320 acres of land to any man who cultivated land in the Oregon Territory for four consecutive years.
6. T F The Oregon Trail actually ended in San Francisco, California.

Name/Date _____

Pacific States 7

Use a current almanac or Internet site to complete a chart for the five Pacific states on another sheet of paper. Include the state's nickname, area in square miles, population, and people per square mile.

Name/Date _____

Pacific States 8

All of the Pacific states contain active and/or inactive volcanoes. Define these terms on another sheet of paper.

1. magma
2. lava
3. volcanic crater
4. dormant
5. Vulcan
6. caldera
7. volcanology
8. submarine volcano

Name/Date _____

Pacific States 9

Answer these questions on your own paper.

1. What is the Pacific Flyway?

2. Earthquakes occur often in the Pacific states. What is the relationship between tectonic plates and earthquakes?

Name/Date _____

Pacific States 10

Match the description to the correct mountain.

____ 1. Mauna Kea   ____ 2. Mt. Hood
____ 3. Mt. Whitney   ____ 4. Mt. McKinley
____ 5. Mt. Rainier

A. Highest mountain in Washington
B. Highest mountain in Alaska
C. Highest mountain in Oregon
D. Highest mountain in Hawaii
E. Highest mountain in California

Geography Warm-ups: The West Pacific States (Appendix Map #10)

Name/Date _____

Pacific States 11

1. _____ began as a fur trading post in 1811 and became the first permanent settlement in Oregon.

2. _____ is known as the Evergreen State.

3. _____ are carved wooden logs decorated with painted carvings, often of animals, by Native Americans along the Pacific coast.

Name/Date _____

Pacific States 12

On another sheet of paper, write a short description of each of these places in California.

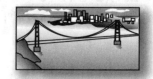

1. Palomar Observatory
2. Golden Gate Bridge
3. Redwood National Park
4. Sequoia National Park
5. Yosemite National Park
6. Mohave Desert

Name/Date _____

Pacific States 13

Circle "T" for true or "F" for false.

1. T   F   John Jay Fossil Beds National Monument contains fossils of saber-toothed tigers, giant pigs, three-toed horses, and other animals that lived long ago.

2. T   F   Mount Olympus in Washington was named for the mythical home of the Greek god of the underworld.

3. T   F   Much is known about the Makah people in Washington because a mudslide covered most of a village about 500 years ago, preserving details of their everyday lives.

4. T   F   James Marshall found the first gold nuggets in 1848 that started the California Gold Rush.

5. T   F   Bristlecone pines in California are the oldest known trees on Earth.

Name/Date _____

Pacific States 14

Write your answers on another sheet of paper.

1. Oregon is rich in gold, silver, iron, copper, and bauxite. For what is bauxite used?

2. The Oregon state quarter depicts Crater Lake. What is unique about Crater Lake?

3. Use a map scale to estimate the distance from Portland, Oregon, to Portland, Maine.

4. What types of marine animals provide the basis for the commercial fishing industry in Oregon?

Name/Date _____

Pacific States 15

Write your answers on another sheet of paper.

1. Grand Coulee Dam was built on the Columbia River and produces hydroelectric power. What is *hydroelectric power*?

2. What happened to the Tacoma Narrows Bridge in 1940?

3. What did the slogan "Fifty-four forty, or fight" mean?

4. What is the Space Needle?

Geography Warm-ups: The West Pacific States (Appendix Map #10)

Name/Date _____

Pacific States 16

Match these states with their state fish.

_____ 1. Humuhumunukunukuapua'a

_____ 2. Garibaldi

_____ 3. King salmon

_____ 4. Steelhead trout

_____ 5. Chinook salmon

A. Washington   B. Oregon   C. Hawaii

D. California   E. Alaska

Name/Date _____

Pacific States 17

Write your answers on another sheet of paper.

1. The rugged Alaska coastline includes many fjords. What are fjords?

2. There are more than 100,000 glaciers in Alaska. What is a glacier?

3. Why was Alaska called Seward's Folly and Seward's Icebox?

4. What is the origin of the word *Alaska*?

Name/Date _____

Pacific States 18

Based on climate, cross out the animals not likely to be found living in Alaska or its surrounding waters.

whales	moose	caribou
Kodiak bears	lizards	polar bears
martens	minks	tigers
mountain goats	wolves	coyotes
alligators	otters	beavers
sea lions	camels	harbor seals
sea otters		

Name/Date _____

Pacific States 19

List the seven main islands of Hawaii in order by size. Include the nickname(s) and the official color of each island.

1. _____

2. _____

3. _____

4. _____

5. _____

6. _____

7. _____

Name/Date _____

Pacific States 20

Circle "T" for true or "F" for false.

1. T F Hawaii became the 49th state in 1959.

2. T F Mauna Loa is the most active volcano on Earth.

3. T F Hawaii contains about 50 islands in all.

4. T F The first people to settle in Hawaii traveled about 2,000 miles over the ocean in canoes.

5. T F Captain Cook named the islands the Sandwich Islands in 1778.

Geography Warm-ups: Appendix Map #1
The United States

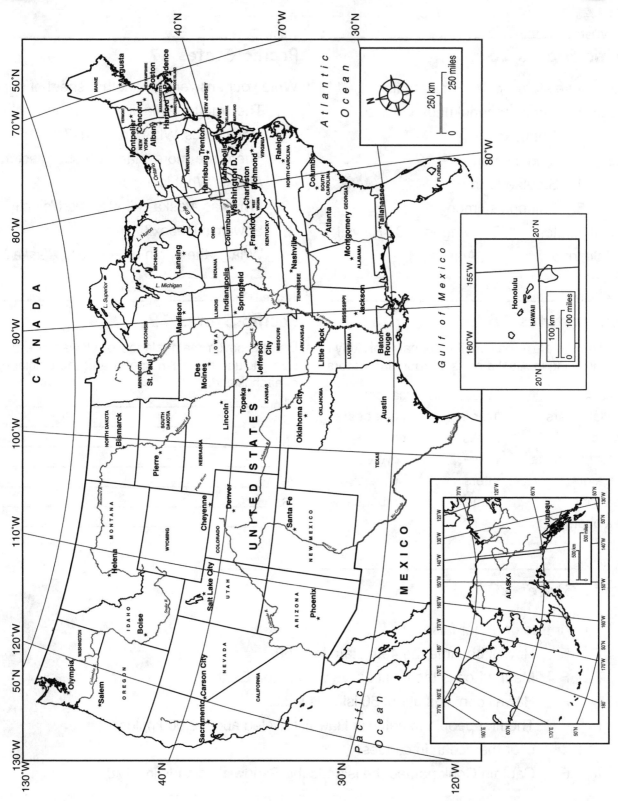

Geography Warm-ups: Appendix Map #2
The Northeast—New England States

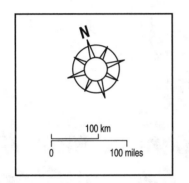

Geography Warm-ups: Appendix Map #3
The Northeast—Middle Atlantic States

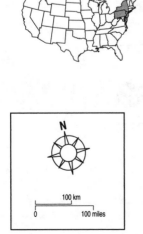

31

Geography Warm-ups: Appendix Map #4
The Midwest—East North Central States

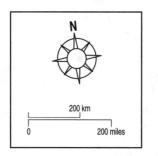

Geography Warm-ups: Appendix Map #5
The Midwest—West North Central States

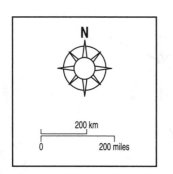

32

Geography Warm-ups: Appendix Map #6
The South—South Atlantic States

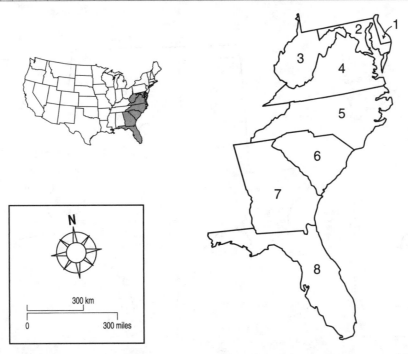

N

300 km

0   300 miles

Geography Warm-ups: Appendix Map #7
The South—East South Central States

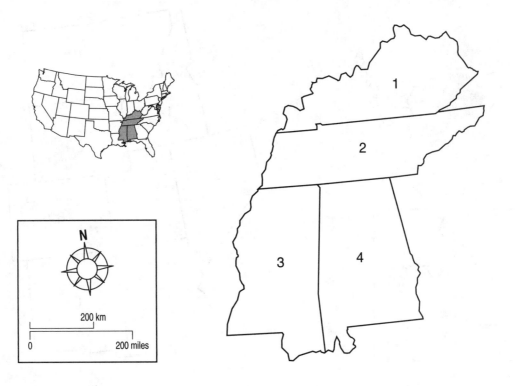

N

200 km

0   200 miles

33

Geography Warm-ups: Appendix Map #8
The South—West South Central States

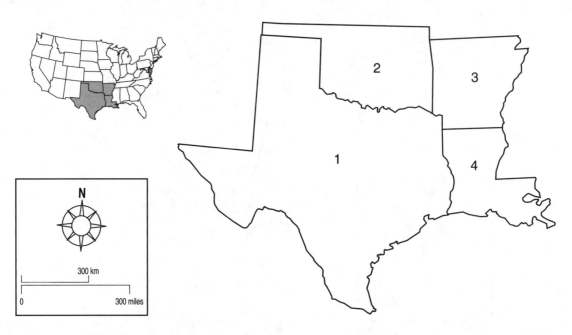

Geography Warm-ups: Appendix Map #9
The West—Mountain States

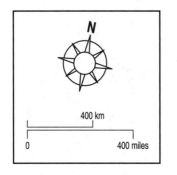

34

Geography Warm-ups: Appendix Map #10
The West—Pacific States

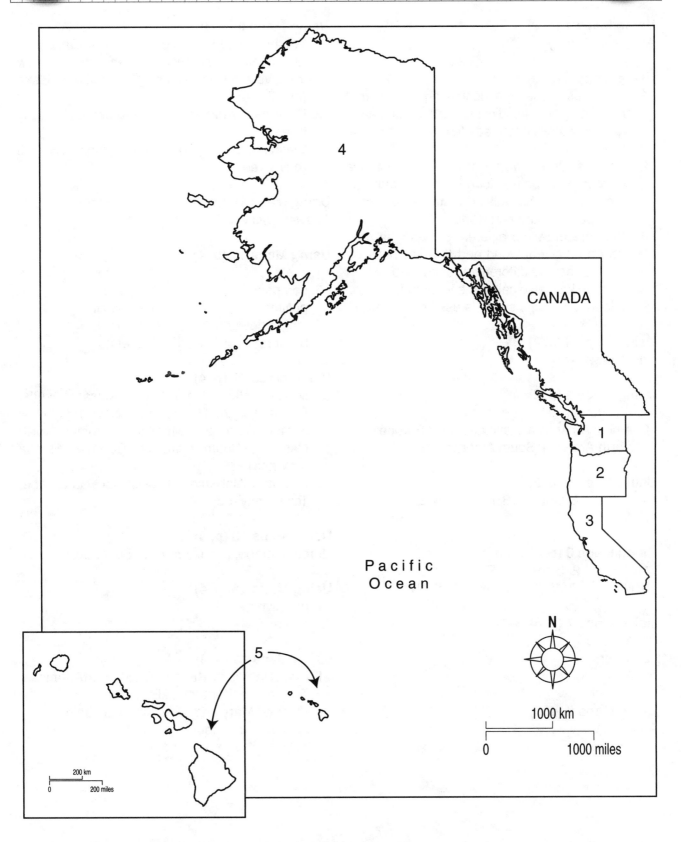

CANADA

1

2

3

Pacific
Ocean

N

1000 km

0   1000 miles

5

200 km

0   200 miles

Geography Warm-ups: Answer Keys

Using Maps 1 (p. 2)
Answers will vary.

Using Maps 2 (p. 2)
1. A compass rose is a design on a map that shows direction. It indicates north, south, east, west, as well as intermediate directions on the map.
2. A map scale shows the ratio of the distance between two points found on the map as compared to the actual distance between these points in the real world.
3. Maps are drawn to different scales. The ratio between the real world and the distances on the map may be different for each map.
4. The map key (also called the legend) is a small table that explains symbols used on the map.

Using Maps 3 (p. 2)
Answers will vary.

Using Maps 4 (p. 2)
1. A continent is a large landmass.
2. Africa; Antarctica; Asia; Australia; Europe; North America; South America

Using Maps 5 (p. 2)
1. B   2. C   3. D   4. E
5. A

Using Maps 6 (p. 3)
1. N   2. SW   3. E   4. S
5. NE   6. W   7. NE   8. NW

Using Maps 7 (p. 3)
1. Arizona
2. water
3. 20

Using Maps 8 (p. 3)
Answers will vary.

Using Maps 9 (p. 3)
1. Washington; Idaho; Montana; North Dakota; Minnesota; Michigan; Ohio; Pennsylvania; New York; Vermont; New Hampshire; Maine; Alaska (any three)
2. California; Arizona; New Mexico; Texas (any three)
3. Washington; Oregon; California; Alaska; Hawaii (any three)

Using Maps 10 (p. 3)
Answers will vary.

Using Maps 11 (p. 4)
1. scale   2. latitude
3. compass   4. legend
5. political   6. physical
7. longitude   8. degrees
9. borders   10. oceans

Using Maps 12 (p. 4)
1. Maine, New Hampshire, Massachusetts, Rhode Island, Connecticut, New York, New Jersey, Delaware, Maryland, Virginia, North Carolina, South Carolina, Georgia, Florida (any four)
2. Florida, Alabama, Mississippi, Louisiana, Texas (any four)

Using Maps 13 (p. 4)
Huron, Ontario, Michigan, Erie, Superior

Using Maps 14 (p. 4)
1. northwest
2. south

Using Maps 15 (p. 4)
1. Iowa, Nebraska, Kansas, Oklahoma, Arkansas, Tennessee, Kentucky, Illinois (any four)
2. Virginia, Maryland, Pennsylvania, Ohio, Kentucky (any four)

The Northeast—New England 1 (p. 5)
1. Maine   2. Vermont
3. New Hampshire   4. Massachusetts
5. Connecticut   6. Rhode Island

The Northeast—New England 2 (p. 5)
1. Augusta   2. Montpelier
3. Concord   4. Boston
5. Hartford   6. Providence

The Northeast—New England 3 (p. 5)
1. New Hampshire
2. Rhode Island
3. Massachusetts
4. Vermont

The Northeast—New England 4 (p. 5)
Most of the early settlers came from England.

The Northeast—New England 5 (p. 5)
1. Canada
2. Maine
3. Atlantic Ocean
4. Rhode Island

The Northeast—New England 6 (p. 6)
1. D   2. A   3. F   4. E
5. B   6. C

The Northeast—New England 7 (p. 6)
1. A cape is a pointed piece of land that sticks out into a sea, ocean, lake, or river.
2. Massachusetts: Cape Cod
3. The English explorer Bartholomew Gosnold named it Cape Cod in 1602 because of the abundance of codfish in the surrounding waters.

The Northeast—New England 8 (p. 6)
1. Appalachian Mountains
2. New Brunswick
3. New England clam chowder

The Northeast—New England 9 (p. 6)
Cross out palm, grapefruit, bamboo, and orchids.

The Northeast—New England 10 (p. 6)
Reports will vary.

The Northeast—New England 11 (p. 7)
1. F   2. F   3. T   4. T
5. T

The Northeast—New England 12 (p. 7)
1. Quebec
2. The Old Man of the Mountain
3. It was destroyed by a rockslide.

The Northeast—New England 13 (p. 7)
1. green mountain
2. Revolutionary War
3. Connecticut River

The Northeast—New England 14 (p. 7)
1. A community governed by a church
2. Bridgeport, Connecticut
3. New Haven

The Northeast—New England 15 (p. 7)
Answers will vary.

The Northeast—Middle Atlantic States 1 (p. 8)
1. New York: Albany
2. Pennsylvania: Harrisburg
3. New Jersey: Trenton

The Northeast—Middle Atlantic States 2 (p. 8)
1. New York
2. West Virginia, Maryland, Delaware, and New Jersey
3. Lake Ontario and Lake Erie

The Northeast—Middle Atlantic States 3 (p. 8)
1. Climate is the pattern of weather for a region over a long period of time.
2. deer, raccoons, eagles, turkeys, frogs

The Northeast—Middle Atlantic States 4 (p. 8)
1. New York
2. colder
3. Delaware River

The Northeast—Middle Atlantic States 5 (p. 8)
1. Philadelphia
2. Fort Pitt
3. Commonwealth of Pennsylvania
4. William Penn
5. Penn's woods

The Northeast—Middle Atlantic States 6 (p. 9)
1. New Amsterdam
2. New York City
3. Long Island
4. Central Park

The Northeast—Middle Atlantic States 7 (p. 9)
1. D   2. E   3. B   4. C
5. A

The Northeast—Middle Atlantic States 8 (p. 9)
Songs will vary.

The Northeast—Middle Atlantic States 9 (p. 9)
Pennsylvania: motto, Virtue, Liberty, and Independence; flower, mountain laurel; tree, eastern hemlock; animal, white-tailed deer; bird, ruffed grouse; insect, firefly
New Jersey: motto, Liberty and Prosperity; flower, purple violet; tree, red oak; animal, horse; bird, eastern goldfinch; insect, honeybee
New York: motto, Excelsior; flower, rose; tree, sugar maple; animal, beaver; bird, eastern bluebird; insect, none

The Northeast—Middle Atlantic States 10 (p. 9)
1. Leni Lenape
2. The Netherlands (Holland)
3. Aaron Burr
4. Trenton

The Midwest—East North Central States 1 (p. 10)
1. Wisconsin   2. Illinois
3. Michigan   4. Indiana
5. Ohio

The Midwest—East North Central States 2 (p. 10)
1. Madison   2. Springfield
3. Lansing   4. Indianapolis
5. Columbus

The Midwest—East North Central States 3 (p. 10)
Answers will vary.

The Midwest—East North Central States 4 (p. 10)
1. Michigan
2. Ohio
3. Illinois
4. Wisconsin and Illinois

The Midwest—East North Central States 5 (p. 10)
1. A peninsula is a body of land surrounded by water on three sides.
2. Michigan
3. Wisconsin

The Midwest—East North Central States 6 (p. 11)
1. Lakes Superior, Michigan, Huron, and Erie
2. Lake Ontario
3. Lake Superior
4. Lake Ontario
5. Lake Michigan
6. Canada

The Midwest—East North Central States 7 (p. 11)
1. The Great Lakes formed when glaciers scraped the earth during the last Ice Age.
2. A lake is a large body of water surrounded by land on all sides.
3. These five lakes are the largest in the United States and among the largest anywhere on Earth.

The Midwest—East North Central States 8 (p. 11)
1. Between 1,200 and 1,300 miles. Allow flexibility in answers.
2. Portage means to carry the canoe over land for a short distance to avoid currents and obstacles, such as waterfalls and rapids, or to go from one body of water to another.
3. animal furs

The Midwest—East North Central States 9 (p. 11)
1. Chicago, IL
2. Detroit, MI
3. Canton, OH
4. False

**The Midwest—East North Central States 10
(p. 11)**
Answers will vary.

**The Midwest—East North Central States 11
(p. 12)**
1. Ohio   2. Cincinnati   3. Akron
4. Toledo   5. Dayton

**The Midwest—East North Central States 12
(p. 12)**
1. Land of the Indians
2. auto industry
3. Evansville
4. Wabash River

**The Midwest—East North Central States 13
(p. 12)**
1. 10 stories
2. The Mississippians

**The Midwest—East North Central States 14
(p. 12)**
1. Ottawa
2. F (*Michigan* means "great water.")
3. A strait is a narrow passage of water connecting
   two larger bodies of water.

**The Midwest—East North Central States 15
(p. 12)**
1. America's Dairyland and Badger State
2. Lake Winnebago
3. the Fox

**The Midwest—West North Central States 1
(p. 13)**
1. North Dakota   2. South Dakota
3. Nebraska   4. Kansas
5. Minnesota   6. Iowa
7. Missouri

**The Midwest—West North Central States 2
(p. 13)**
1. Bismarck   2. Pierre
3. Lincoln   4. Topeka
5. St. Paul   6. Des Moines
7. Jefferson City

**The Midwest—West North Central States 3
(p. 13)**
1. F   2. T   3. F   4. T
5. T

**The Midwest—West North Central States 4
(p. 13)**
1. A plain is a large area of land characterized
   by flat to gently sloping land, often a grassland
   with few trees.
2. There are few trees for lumber.
3. A sod house is constructed almost entirely
   of large chunks of earth, cut like "bricks" and
   piled up to form walls as much as three to four
   feet thick.

**The Midwest—West North Central States 5
(p. 13)**
1. Minnesota
2. Missouri River
3. Gulf of Mexico
4. Minnesota

**The Midwest—West North Central States 6
(p. 14)**
Circle these crops: wheat, apples, soybeans,
corn, potatoes, cabbage, and hay.

**The Midwest—West North Central States 7
(p. 14)**
1. Minnesota   2. Kansas
3. Nebraska   4. South Dakota
5. North Dakota   6. Missouri
7. Iowa

**The Midwest—West North Central States 8
(p. 14)**
1. G   2. F   3. A   4. C
5. E   6. B   7. D

**The Midwest—West North Central States 9
(p. 14)**
1. Nebraska's climate includes winter temperatures below 0°F and summer temperatures as
   high as the lower 100°sF. There are four dis-
   tinct seasons with most precipitation occurring
   between April and September. Blizzards are
   common in winter, with tornadoes and severe
   storms, with damaging winds, hail, and heavy
   rains during the year.

2. Fort Atkinson
3. In 1917 near Omaha, NE
4. flat river or broad water

The Midwest—West North Central States 10 (p. 14)
1. December 28, 1846
2. and 3. Answers will vary.
4. True
5. True

The Midwest—West North Central States 11 (p. 15)
1. B   2. C   3. D   4. A

The Midwest—West North Central States 12 (p. 15)
1. Mark Twain (Samuel Clemens)
2. New Madrid
3. St. Joseph, MO
4. A plateau is a very large elevated land formation with a relatively flat top.

The Midwest—West North Central States 13 (p. 15)
1. ND   2. SD   3. SD   4. SD
5. ND   6. ND & SD   7. ND   8. ND
9. SD   10. SD

The Midwest—West North Central States 14 (p. 15)
1. A cave is a chamber beneath the surface of the earth or in the side of a hill, cliff, or mountain.
2. Caves range in size from small hillside openings to subterranean systems that extend for many miles underground and may have many outlets.
3. Limestone is a type of rock composed of minerals that are relatively soluble in water.
4. Limestone caves form when limestone rock is dissolved away by water over the course of many years.
5. Stalactites are mineral deposits. They hang like icicles from the roofs of caves.
6. Stalagmites are mineral deposits. They extend upward from the cave floors.

The Midwest—West North Central States 15 (p. 15)
Answers will vary.

The South—South Atlantic States 1 (p. 16)
1. Delaware   2. Maryland
3. West Virginia   4. Virginia
5. North Carolina   6. South Carolina
7. Georgia   8. Florida
9. *Florida and *West Virginia

The South—South Atlantic States 2 (p. 16)
1. Dover   2. Annapolis
3. Charleston   4. Richmond
5. Raleigh   6. Columbia
7. Atlanta   8. Tallahassee

The South—South Atlantic States 3 (p. 16)
1. T   2. F (Hawaii is farther south)
3. F (between Virginia and South Carolina)

The South—South Atlantic States 4 (p. 16)
1. Maryland and Virginia
2. A bay is an area of water bordered by land on three sides.
3. Florida
4. A gulf is a part of an ocean or sea that is partly surrounded by land. (It's usually larger than a bay.)
5. The Florida Keys are a chain of islands, islets, and reefs between the Straits of Florida and Florida Bay.

The South—South Atlantic States 5 (p. 16)
1. Washington, D.C.
2. Answers will vary. Someplace in Kansas or Nebraska would be centrally located.
3. False (District of Columbia)
4. It's a park.
5. Potomac River
6. False

The South—South Atlantic States 6 (p. 17)
1. Maryland   2. Virginia
3. North Carolina   4. Georgia
5. South Carolina   6. North Carolina

The South—South Atlantic States 7 (p. 17)

1. West Virginia
2. The Appalachian Mountains
3. The Allegheny Mountains
4. Coal is a type of rock formed from plants that died millions of years ago in ancient tropical swamps. As layers of mud, sand, and vegetation accumulated, pressure and heat reduced the water content, leaving a high percent of carbon.

The South—South Atlantic States 8 (p. 17)

1. Wilmington
2. It was the first to ratify the U.S. Constitution.
3. Sweden

The South—South Atlantic States 9 (p. 17)

1. Queen Henrietta Maria, wife of King Charles I of England
2. A straight line determined by two surveyors, Charles Mason and Jeremiah Dixon, to settle border disputes between Pennsylvania and Maryland colonists.
3.

The South—South Atlantic States 10 (p. 17)

1. North Carolina
2. Roanoke Island
3. South Carolina
4. Florida
5. A sound is an area of a sea or ocean mostly surrounded by land.

The South—South Atlantic States 11 (p. 18)

1. F   2. C   3. D   4. B
5. E   6. A

The South—South Atlantic States 12 (p. 18)

1. Virginia   2. 1863
3. They are shaped somewhat like the handles of a pan.
4. He hoped to end the conflicts between settlers and Native Americans.

The South—South Atlantic States 13 (p. 18)

1. While I Breathe, I Hope
2. yellow jessamine
3. Carolina wren
4. peach
5. milk
6. The shag
7. Boykin spaniel
8. Carolina mantid
9. loggerhead turtle
10. striped bass
11. blue granite
12. wild turkey

The South—South Atlantic States 14 (p. 18)

1. T
2. T
3. F (300 miles long and 230 miles wide)
4. T

The South—South Atlantic States 15 (p. 18)

1. Big Cypress Swamp and the Everglades
2. Lists will vary.
3. Seminoles

The South—East South Central States 1 (p. 19)

1. Kentucky: Frankfort
2. Tennessee: Nashville
3. Mississippi: Jackson
4. Alabama: Montgomery

The South—East South Central States 2 (p. 19)

1. Mississippi & Alabama
2. Kentucky, Tennessee, & Mississippi
3. Ohio, Indiana, Illinois, Missouri, Tennessee, Virginia, & West Virginia
4. Kentucky
5. Ohio River

The South—East South Central States 3 (p. 19)

1. A. Lexington   B. Louisville
2. A. Chattanooga   B. Memphis
3. A. Huntsville   B. Birmingham
4. A. Natchez   B. Biloxi

The South—East South Central States 4
(p. 19)
1. 1819　　2. 1792　　3. 1817
4. 1796　　5. cotton

The South—East South Central States 5
(p. 19)
1. MS　　2. TN　　3. KY　　4. AL
5. KY　　6. AL　　7. TN　　8. MS
9. TN　　10. MS

The South—East South Central States 6
(p. 20)
1. F　　2. T　　3. T

The South—East South Central States 7
(p. 20)
1. A fragrant herb used for seasoning and medicinal purposes
2. The grass is dark green. Bluish-purple blossoms in spring make the grass look blue.
3. A moonbow is like a rainbow, but forms only during the full moon in the mist over the falls.
4. 350 miles

The South—East South Central States 8
(p. 20)
1. The route the Cherokee and many other Native American tribes were forced to take from their homelands to the Indian Territory in Oklahoma
2. They buried their dead in mounds of earth.
3. Sequoyah

The South—East South Central States 9
(p. 20)
1. Wood becomes petrified when trees die in a marshland and are buried by sediment penetrated by water rich in silica. Over millions of years, the wood fibers are replaced by silica and other minerals, and the wood turns to stone.
2. A catfish
3. Bluffs are steep hills or cliffs next to a river.
4. In mourning for the death of Abe Lincoln

The South—East South Central States 10
(p. 20)
1. Spain
2. Creek tribe
3. Choctaw
4. Montgomery, Alabama
5. Jefferson Davis

The South—West South Central States 1
(p. 21)
1. Texas: Austin
2. Oklahoma: Oklahoma City
3. Arkansas: Little Rock
4. Louisiana: Baton Rouge

The South—West South Central States 2
(p. 21)
1. Hurricane Katrina (also Hurricane Rita)
2. A tornado develops over land and is a violently rotating column of air originating in a thundercloud and extending to the ground, characterized by swirling winds in excess of 75 miles per hour. A hurricane develops over water and consists of high-velocity winds blowing around a low-pressure center, known as the eye of the storm. To be classified as a hurricane, the storm must have sustained winds over 74 miles per hour.

The South—West South Central States 3
(p. 21)
1. Oklahoma
2. Great river
3. Texas
4. France
5. One explanation is that the name referred to a red cypress tree that marked the boundaries between the hunting grounds of two Native American tribes.

The South—West South Central States 4
(p. 21)
1. Gulf of Mexico
2. Texas
3. Mexico
4. parishes

The South—West South Central States 5 (p. 21)
1. A mesa is a hill with a flat top and at least one side that is a steep cliff.
2. Ouachita Mountains, Arbuckle Mountains, Wichita Mountains
3. Red River
4. bison, bullfrog, white bass, scissor-tailed flycatcher, redbud

The South—West South Central States 6 (p. 22)
1. C   2. D   3. B   4. E
5. A

The South—West South Central States 7 (p. 22)
1. A razorback is a thin, long-legged wild hog found in Arkansas.
2. Crater of Diamonds State Park is near Murfreesboro, Arkansas.
3. A hot spring is a natural flow of hot water from the ground in a specific area. The water at Hot Springs National Park remains near 143°F throughout the year.

The South—West South Central States 8 (p. 22)
1. T   2. T   3. F (Alaska)
4. F (Dallas and Austin are not port cities.)
5. T

The South—West South Central States 9 (p. 22)
1. Stephen Austin
2. 1836; Sam Houston; almost 10 years

The South—West South Central States 10 (p. 22)
1. A delta is an area of low, watery land formed at the mouth of a river from the silt, sand, and small rocks that flow downstream and are deposited there.
2. Wetlands occur in low-lying areas near bodies of water where the water table is usually at, above, or just below the land surface. Marshes, swamps, and bayous are types of wetlands.

3. A bayou is a small secondary river that feeds into larger bodies of water. The area is characterized by slow-moving streams that wander through marshes and lowlands.
4. Sea level is the average height, or elevation, of the sea surface as measured over time. Geographers use sea level as a benchmark for measuring land elevation.

The West—Mountain States 1 (p. 23)
1. Idaho   2. Montana
3. Wyoming   4. Nevada
5. Utah   6. Colorado
7. Arizona   8. New Mexico

The West—Mountain States 2 (p. 23)
1. Boise   2. Helena
3. Cheyenne   4. Carson City
5. Salt Lake City   6. Denver
7. Phoenix   8. Santa Fe

The West—Mountain States 3 (p. 23)
1. Montana   2. Arizona
3. Utah   4. New Mexico
5. Idaho   6. Wyoming
7. Nevada   8. Colorado

The West—Mountain States 4 (p. 23)
1. Arizona and New Mexico
2. Arizona
3. Utah
4. Montana and Idaho
5. Mostly in Wyoming, partially in Montana and Idaho

The West—Mountain States 5 (p. 23)
1. A canyon is a deep valley with very steep sides often carved through rock by a river.
2. State borders that are straight lines are determined by surveyors. Most state borders are not straight because they follow natural boundaries, such as rivers, lakes, or mountains.
3. The Rocky Mountains
4. Nevada and Idaho

The West—Mountain States 6 (p. 24)
1. At the point where four states meet: Utah, Colorado, Arizona, and New Mexico
2. Yellowstone National Park
3. Mesa Verde in Colorado
4. Devil's Tower National Monument in Wyoming

The West—Mountain States 7 (p. 24)
1. CO   2. ID & NV   3. AZ   4. NM
5. UT   6. WY and MT

The West—Mountain States 8 (p. 24)
1. 1890
2. potatoes
3. silver
4. huckleberry

The West—Mountain States 9 (p. 24)
1. T
2. T
3. F (Alaska has the lowest population density.)
4. F (Chinooks are the warm winds that blow in late winter and early spring.)
5. F (about 630 miles long)

The West—Mountain States 10 (p. 24)
A geyser is a type of hot spring that erupts periodically, ejecting a column of hot water and steam into the air.

Mud pots are formed in high-temperature geothermal areas when a small amount of water causes mud to bubble to the surface. The boiling mud often squirts over the brim of the mud pot and a mini-volcano builds up, sometimes reaching three to five feet high.

Fumaroles are openings in Earth's crust that emit steam and gases such as carbon dioxide, sulfur dioxide, hydrochloric acid, and hydrogen sulfide.

The West—Mountain States 11 (p. 25)
1. The Mormons
2. A small amount of dissolved salts, leached from the soil and rocks, is deposited into Great Salt Lake every year by rivers that flow into the lake. Because it lacks outlets or drainage, natural water loss occurs only through evaporation, which leaves high concentrates of dissolved salts.

3. The walls of the canyons in this area are sandstone. Over millions of years, the rock has been sculpted by wind and erosion.
4. The arches and bridges were formed from sandstone carved out of an ancient seabed. Erosion, caused by water freezing, thawing, and flooding, produced these giant stone formations.

The West—Mountain States 12 (p. 25)
1. T   2. F (Not until 1858)   3. T

The West—Mountain States 13 (p. 25)
1. The phoenix was a mythical bird that lived for 500 years before being consumed by fire. Out of the fire arose a new, young phoenix.
2. Answers will vary.
3. Pueblos are multi-story apartment-like dwellings built of adobe bricks or rocks covered with adobe. Usually built in terraces, the people used ladders to reach different levels, with access often being in the roofs. Frequently built against cliff walls, this type of dwelling makes use of materials available in the area, provides shade and coolness during the heat of the day, and offers a defensive position in case of attack.

The West—Mountain States 14 (p. 25)
1. Adobe is a building material made by mixing certain types of soil and water with straw, and then dried in the sun.
2. A kiva is an underground or partly underground chamber, usually with a hole at the top that lets in daylight, used by some Native American groups for ceremonies or formal meetings.
3. A petroglyph is a prehistoric drawing done on rock.
4. Carlsbad Caverns in New Mexico is an extensive system of over 100 known beautiful limestone caves famous for the huge number of bats that dwell there.
5. Javalinas are a type of wild boar.
6. The piñon tree is a type of pine tree that produces a small, sweet, edible nut.
7. A butte is a flat-topped rock or hill formation with steep sides.
8. A saguaro is a large, slow-growing cactus (up to 60 feet high), with upward-curving branches and edible red fruit.

The West—Mountain States 15 (p. 25)

1. It is a large artificial lake formed when Hoover Dam was built on the Colorado River.
2. Sierra Nevada Range
3. Reports will vary.

The West—Pacific States 1 (p. 26)

1. Washington: Olympia
2. Oregon: Salem
3. California: Sacramento
4. Alaska: Juneau
5. Hawaii: Honolulu

The West—Pacific States 2 (p. 26)

1. Alaska and Hawaii
2. Alaska
3. south
4. northeast

The West—Pacific States 3 (p. 26)

1. Columbia River
2. Alaska and California
3. Alaska and Washington
4. California

The West—Pacific States 4 (p. 26)

1. HI   2. AK   3. HI
4. AK, CA, OR, WA
5. AK, WA, CA   6. CA

The West—Pacific States 5 (p. 26)

1. AK   2. WA   3. HI   4. AK
5. AK   6. OR   7. CA   8. WA
9. WA   10. OR   11. HI   12. WA

The West—Pacific States 6 (p. 27)

1. F (Barrow, Alaska)   2. T   3. T
4. F (California)   5. T   6. F

The West—Pacific States 7 (p. 27)

Population and population density will depend on most current statistics available.

Alaska	Last Frontier	656,424 sq. mi.
California	Golden State	163,707 sq. mi.
Hawaii	Aloha State	10,932 sq. mi.
Oregon	Beaver State	98,386 sq. mi.
Washington	Evergreen State	71,303 sq. mi.

The West—Pacific States 8 (p. 27)

1. Magma - molten rock that forms beneath the earth's surface
2. Lava - magma that breaks the surface of the earth and erupts from a volcano
3. Volcanic crater - a roughly circular basin from which magma erupts as gases, lava, and ejecta
4. Dormant – inactive for a long period of time
5. Vulcan – the god of fire in Roman mythology
6. Caldera - a round or oval-shaped low-lying area formed when the ground collapses because of explosive volcanic eruptions
7. Volcanology – the study of the processes, products, hazards, and environmental impacts of volcanic eruptions.
8. Submarine volcano – a volcano that erupts under water. Over time it may form an island.

The West—Pacific States 9 (p. 27)

1. The Pacific Flyway is one of the major seasonal migration routes in North America for many types of birds. It extends from northeastern Alaska south to southern California.
2. Tectonic plates are large blocks of the earth's crust that move slowly across the surface of the planet. When they collide and grind against each other, they generate friction, creating tremendous amounts of energy, which causes severe earthquakes.

The West—Pacific States 10 (p. 27)

1. D   2. C   3. E   4. B
5. A

The West—Pacific States 11 (p. 28)

1. Astoria
2. Washington
3. Totem poles

The West—Pacific States 12 (p. 28)

Answers will vary.

The West—Pacific States 13 (p. 28)

1. T   2. F   3. T   4. T
5. T

The West—Pacific States 14 (p. 28)

1. Bauxite is a mineral most widely used in the production of aluminum.
2. Crater Lake is the deepest lake in the nation (1,932 feet). It formed about 6,000 years ago when Mount Mazam erupted. The water is a deep, brilliant blue.
3. About 3,200 miles
4. Salmon, tuna, flounder, crabs, shrimp, oysters, rockfish, sturgeon

The West—Pacific States 15 (p. 28)

1. Hydroelectric power is electricity produced by water. Most hydroelectric power comes from the energy of dammed water driving a water turbine and generator.
2. Wind caused vibrations, making it sway, twist, buckle, and finally collapse.
3. For a time, the boundary between Canada and the United States west of Minnesota was in dispute. Americans, who wanted to go to war with Britain if the boundary was not set at 54 degrees, 40 minutes north latitude, used this slogan. Eventually a compromise set the boundary at the 49th parallel in 1818.
4. The Space Needle is a landmark in Seattle built for the 1962 World's Fair. It is a 650-foot high tower with a revolving restaurant and gift shop near the top.

The West—Pacific States 16 (p. 29)

1. C   2. D   3. E   4. A
5. B

The West—Pacific States 17 (p. 29)

1. Fjords are deep, narrow inlets that have been gouged out by glaciers and then partly submerged by the sea.
2. Glaciers are huge accumulations of ice, snow, water, rock, and sediment that move slowly because of gravity. Glaciers form when temperatures are low enough to allow snow to accumulate and slowly transform into ice.
3. When Secretary of State William Seward arranged for the purchase of Alaska from Russia in 1867 for 7.2 million dollars, many people thought it was a waste of money.
4. Alaska comes from the Aleut word *aláxsxaq,* loosely translated as "great land."

The West—Pacific States 18 (p. 29)

Cross off: lizards, tigers, alligators, camels

The West—Pacific States 19 (p. 29)

1. Hawai'i = Big Island (red)
2. Maui = Valley Isle (pink)
3. Moloka'i = Friendly Island (green)
4. Lana'i = Pineapple Island (orange)
5. O'ahu = Gathering Place (yellow)
6. Kaua'i = Garden Island (purple)
7. Ni'ihau = Forbidden Island (white)

The West—Pacific States 20 (p. 29)

1. F (50th)   2. T   3. F (132)
4. T   5. T